180°
Life Leadership

Elise Krentzel   Cassie Lincoln

180° Life Leadership
Elise Krentzel & Cassie Lincoln

ISBN Paperback: 979-8-9918136-3-1
ISBN Ebook: 979-8-9918136-4-8

Published by
Kumi Books

Table of Contents

A Word From the Authors

Cassie Lincoln and Elise Krentzel met roughly one year ago on a social media platform, and they hit it off so quickly that the two jumped onto a Zoom call. It was an instant connection. Less than a month later, Cassie introduced Elise to one of her clients, who became one of hers. Talk about efficiency! But then, things got... interesting. They fell out. To this day, it's hard to pinpoint why—tension crept into the relationship, and let's just say it wasn't their best chapter.

Fast forward to a press conference. Circumstances reunited the women, and something happened. Call it fate, timing, or just sheer stubbornness, but suddenly, the ice broke. Cassie, hesitant to warm up to Elise at first, held back—unsure if they could genuinely align. At the same time, Cassie decided that the tension between them was counterproductive and let her guard down. Elise realized she respected Cassie's brilliant way with the written word and genuinely liked her. Against all odds, Elise proposed working together. And to her utter shock (and relief), Cassie said yes.

United as partners, here they are now, blending their unique perspectives to make the world a better place. Together, they aim to help their colleagues improve their lives through lessons they each learned the hard way.

Many of the quotes in this book trace their roots back to Elise's first book, Under My Skin: Drama, Trauma, and Rock 'n' Roll. With her uncanny ability to laser-focus and Cassie's knack for distilling her life experiences into bite-sized wisdom, these hard-earned words of insight are yours to reflect upon, share, and use.

They've both grown throughout their lives, but in 2024, it felt like warp speed. In their own words, the very ones that guided each of them toward a harmonious relationship, they decided to share with you how to transform your life by simply meditating on these quotes. They proved the impossible is possible when you adhere to the friendly voice inside.

Elise Krentzel & Cassie Lincoln

Personal Growth and Self-Awareness

It takes a long time to be on time.

I used to be a drama queen,
but now I'm just a queen.

Self-respect begins with knowing.
The "no" in knowing is your best friend.

Staying true to yourself is difficult because conformity is such pressure.

Originality is not for generative AI.
No one can replicate you.

Wisdom is knowing when to listen,
step back, or walk away.

You earn self-trust by keeping
the promises you make to yourself.

Growth doesn't shout; it whispers—pay attention to the quiet shifts in your soul.

W hat you envy in others often mirrors
what you've buried in yourself.

Don't measure your life in hours—
measure it in meaning.

Your body and mind always speak—
don't wait until they scream to listen.

Not every problem is yours to solve,
and that's okay.

Confidence and Inner Strength

Have the courage to stand up
for your convictions.

Confidence doesn't shout; it walks in
without asking permission.

I stopped chasing crowns when I realized
I already had one.

Saying no isn't rejection;
it's self-respect in disguise.

You can't fly until you stop holding
your own wings down.

What limits you most isn't outside—
it's what you believe inside.

Resilience isn't about never breaking; it's about finding the strength to rebuild.

Reliance on others without question
is saying, "Take my power."

Mindfulness and

Emotional Intelligence

Thoughts travel faster than light.
Be mindful.

When two people understand each other, they listen without ego bias.

Be like a deer: gentle and sensitive;
not like a bull: headstrong and domineering.

Watch what you put in your mouth; otherwise, regret what comes out.

Fear is a useful emotion; it shows you where to grow stronger.

K indness is never weakness;
it's courage in disguise.

Be at one with yourself—
that's where peace lives.

Life is happening now—

don't miss it staring at a screen.

Philosophy and Wisdom

There is no courage in security—
the true test lies in reality.

Let endings end.
Renewal follows every conclusion.

Live spelled backward is evil.
Live forward.

By doing a 180°, you can see the past or the future but land in the present.

Meaningful work has no clock—
it moves at the speed of purpose.

In a noisy world, silence allows one
to hear the pulse of life.

Integrity is doing what your moral compass knows is right.

Interpersonal Dynamics

Tell no one what to do;
show them how you do it.

If you've met a liar, you'll learn the truth.

Not every relationship is meant to last,
but everyone leaves their mark.

Family isn't always blood;
lifelong bonds don't always start early.

It's not about how many people stand beside you but who truly sees you.

Recognizing your part in a situation is
necessary for forgiveness—first of yourself,
then of others.

Spirituality and Higher Consciousness

Alchemy is when instinct meets magic
in perfect timing.

Self-alignment makes even
the impossible possible.

Being gentle is far stronger than steel.

When you let go of timing,
the perfect momentum carries you forward.

When you stop chasing,
what's meant for you finds you.

Inspiration whispers through kindness, resilience, and joy.

Abundance begins where gratitude lives.

Everything is connected energetically. When you feel bodily pain, it's often tied to unprocessed emotions.

Reflections on Pride and Ego

Pride in unconditional love is real;
pride in your ego is false.

An unchecked ego controls you,
but an examined ego teaches you.

When you understand your ego,
you stop reacting and start healing.

Sometimes, your ego isn't boasting—it's begging you to notice what's been neglected.

Perfectionism stems from a superiority complex hiding inferiority.

About the Authors

Elise Krentzel

Elise Krentzel was born with a flair for words. As a preteen, she discovered her writing talent, starting with diaries and poetry, and in high school, she got published as a music journalist. Her big break came in 1977, touring Japan with KISS before becoming the Tokyo Bureau Chief of Billboard Magazine.

With a career spanning media, communications, and digital publishing, she's never put down the pen—or her curiosity. Think of her as an archeologist for your ideas, unearthing the hidden gems buried in your mind. Through ghostwriting, personalized coaching, publishing services, and online courses, she shapes your treasures into powerful, polished stories. As a storyteller, she finds endless joy in painting vivid canvases for her books and yours.

A world traveler who has lived in 5 countries on 3 continents, Elise currently calls Austin, Texas home. She is the proud mother of one son.

"Writing isn't just my passion—it's the spark that fuels my purpose."

Join the Page-Turner Posse at

https://elisekrentzel.com

About the Authors

Cassie Lincoln

Cassie is a thought leader on business topics, helping entrepreneurs and change makers get momentum in their businesses and lives. With a background in marketing and expertise in sales psychology, she understands how to craft compelling social media presences that deeply resonate with audiences, driving engagement and emotional connection.

As a social media expert with a community of 19,000+ engaged followers, Cassie excels at creating highly engaging, relatable, and viral content that inspires personal and professional growth. Her work empowers mid-career professionals to leave unfulfilling corporate roles, start businesses, and step into lives of purpose and passion.

Cassie is passionate about kindness, resilience, and authenticity, which she weaves into everything she creates. When she's not crafting impactful content or guiding communities, she enjoys exploring philosophy, light hiking, and uncovering the best dining spots near her home in Houston, Texas.

www.ingramcontent.com/pod-product-compliance
Lightning Source LLC
La Vergne TN
LVHW041234080426
835508LV00011B/1211